BOSTON

A PICTURE MEMORY

Text
Bill Harris

Captions
Pauline Graham

Design
Teddy Hartshorn

Photography
Amstock
Colour Library Books Ltd
FPG International
International Stock Photo

Picture Editor
Annette Lerner

Commissioning Editor
Andrew Preston

Publishing Assistant
Edward Doling

Editorial
Jane Adams

Production
Ruth Arthur
Sally Connolly
David Proffit
Andrew Whitelaw

Director of Production
Gerald Hughes

Director of Publishing
David Gibbon

BOSTON
A PICTURE MEMORY

CRESCENT BOOKS
NEW YORK/AVENEL, NEW JERSEY

Perhaps if you were planning a trip to Yellowstone it would be a good idea to include a compass in your backpack. But in Boston, Massachusetts, knowing north from south will probably just confuse you. The city's geographical center is due south of the South End, which itself is west of South Boston. The part of town usually considered to be the central city is up in the northeast corner and the North End is south of East Boston. If you were thinking that landmarks might help you find your way around, bear in mind that Beacon Hill does not tower over the harbor and Back Bay is not a body of water. Street names are not help much either. Five different streets are named for Benjamin Franklin, and just as many for John Adams. Moreover, though the city's main thoroughfare, Washington Street, cuts an honest straight line from northeast to southwest, another one with the same name runs parallel to it for about two miles from northwest to southeast. Don't let it get you down. Getting lost is half the fun of a visit to Boston. There is something to discover around every corner.

Of course, if you have children in tow and you want to impress them with your understanding of the geography of Boston, not to mention your knowledge of American history, the Freedom Trail is just the ticket. It winds a course like the figure eight with the City Hall Visitor Center in the middle, and there are signs to guide you every step of the way from the starting point across from Faneuil Hall and its Marketplace on Dock Square.

Faneuil Hall immortalizes the name of Peter Faneuil, which is more than the stone that was originally put over his grave ever did. The stonecutter, obviously an early student of the reading method called phonics, carved the inscription "P. Funel," which is, indeed, how the name sounds in spite of its spelling. Peter was a nephew of Andrew Faneuil, one of the wealthiest merchants in Boston. When the old man died, he left his entire estate to Peter, except for "five shillings and no more," which he bequeathed to his elder nephew, Benjamin; not because he did not like the boy, but because he had married without Andrew's consent and the old man could not abide his wife. Peter's first and greatest love was fine wine – he had never found a woman with similarly persuasive charms. Predictably, he spent most of his inheritance on wine and brandy, but he also spent a large chunk of it on a produce market with meeting halls upstairs, which he named for himself and donated to the City of Boston. Not long afterward, possibly from sipping all that wine, Peter suddenly dropped dead and his estate, wine cellar and all, went to Benjamin and his wife.

The Hall, which was a favorite meeting place of the Sons of Liberty in the 1760s and early '70s, is still the center of a produce market, and people with causes to consider still gather in the upstairs rooms. But to call Faneuil Hall Marketplace a produce market is like calling Filene's a boutique. You can get a tomato there, but it is likely to be sun dried, and the all-American fare at the food stalls includes chow mein, pizza, tacos and bagels. It also holds a crafts center, containing a collection of shops dispensing high fashion, gifts and souvenirs. About the only thing not easily found there is a place to sit and enjoy the many roving entertainers. The complex of three buildings surrounding the original Faneuil Hall were all built in the mid-1970s and, though they are very good neighbors to the old 1742 building, history hardly stalks its brick and cobblestone plaza with the same presence.

The Freedom Trail walk through Boston's history continues to the site of the Boston Massacre and the Old State House. The Massacre, which happened on March 5, 1770, started when a group of citizens threw stones and snowballs at British soldiers who, exasperated, fired back, killing five of them who became known as the martyrs of State Street. You might have thought that the future President John Adams, a close relative of the firebrand Sam Adams, would very nearly lose his standing as a patriot when he agreed to defend the British officers in court. Instead, by doing so, he set a bench mark for the rule of law when his clients were acquitted. Adams was a prominent lawyer who at the time chose not to be actively involved in politics, and held the respect of Tories and Patriots alike. After the War of Independence he wrote the Bay State's Constitution, which established the government that was run from the Old State House, a 1713 building that had also served the Colonial Government of Massachusetts.

The Old South Meetinghouse, at the other end of the block on the corner of Milk and Washington streets, might escape you if you were expecting a meetinghouse in the style of Faneuil Hall. It looks for all the world like a church, and a very attractive one at that. It is, in fact, one of Boston's oldest church buildings, dating back to 1729 when it replaced another church that had been standing there since 1669. The earlier building was where Benjamin Franklin was baptized on the day he was born in 1706 in a house just down the street. Franklin, of course, had moved on to Philadelphia by the time Sam Adams, John Hancock and others began using the "Old South" for their political meetings. It was here that, on the evening of December 16th, 1773, Sam Adams inspired fellow patriots to put on Indian war paint, board English tea clippers in the nearby harbor and dump their cargoes overboard. During the unpleasantness that followed three years later, British troops occupying the city chopped up the church's pews and pulpit for firewood and turned the remaining open space into a riding academy. After the War, it was converted back into a church. In recent years it has become a museum. Through all that time, the beautiful clock in the belfry has been ticking off the seconds – you can still set your watch by it.

The next stop on the Freedom Trail is one that needs time to be fully appreciated. The Old Corner Bookstore is probably the oldest brick building in Boston, dating back to 1711 when it was built as an apothecary shop by Thomas Crease. It was converted to a bookstore in 1828 by James T. Fields, one of the founders of the venerable old publishing house of Ticknor & Fields which established Boston as the literary center of the United States. Among the writers he brought into print were Henry Wadsworth Longfellow, Ralph Waldo Emerson, Nathaniel Hawthorne, John Greenleaf Whittier, Julia Ward Howe and Harriet Beecher Stowe, who frequently gathered in the store for long afternoons of conversation. The store and the publishing company moved out of the building in 1903, but it has since been restored to some of its nineteenth-century charm as the Globe Corner Bookstore, and it is a perfect place to get reacquainted with the literary and historical giants who once browsed here.

The site upon which the Bookstore was built after the fire of 1711 was already one of historical significance. A young woman named Anne Hutchinson once lived there, having emigrated to Massachusetts from England with her husband in 1634. She scandalized the colony by inviting women into her home to discuss the sermons they had listened to in church each Sunday. Eventually, their discussions began to irritate the clergy because Mrs. Hutchinson had the effrontery to challenge the things they were saying. However, she had plenty of supporters, including Sir Harry Vane – the Governor himself. But the former governor, John Winthrop, was at the head of the opposition and, in the test of wills that followed, Winthrop won. Vane was removed from office and went home to England. Seventy-six businessmen, a healthy percentage of the total number in Boston at the time, were convicted of heresy and forced to turn their guns over to the government. Mrs. Hutchinson and her husband, William, were excommunicated and banished from the colony when she refused to recant. They settled near present-day Pelham Bay on Long Island Sound, where they were killed by Indians a year later in 1643. The edict of banishment was revoked in 1945, more than 300 years after the Hutchinsons left town.

At the same time as Mistress Hutchinson was educating her neighbors, Philemon Pormont was beginning to educate their children down the street at the Boston Latin School, the first public school in America. The institution still exists in the Fenway, and the site of the original is now occupied by a French restaurant in a French-influenced structure that was Boston's City Hall from the Civil War years until the new one was built a few years ago. On its front lawn are statues of Benjamin Franklin and Josiah Quincy, who was Mayor of Boston for five terms. They were both graduates of Boston Latin, as were John Hancock, Samuel Adams, Cotton Mather and others. This school has educated more important men than any other public high school. The statue of Franklin by Robert Greenough, captures the man's personality by showing the left side of his face as that of a philosophical statesman and the right side as the smiling face of the author of *Poor Richard's Almanac.*

The entire block bounded by School, Tremont, Court and Washington Streets was land given to Isaac Johnson, an important passenger aboard the *Arabella*, the ship that brought the first settlers to Boston in 1630. Both he and his wife, Lady Arabella, died during their first winter in the New World and were buried in their own garden. Their neighbors held the couple in such high regard they requested that when they too died, they should be buried as near to Brother Johnson as possible. Their wishes were respected and before long the garden had become a burying ground. In the 1680s, Governor Edmund Andros decided it was time that the Church of England should be established in the colony. But the citizens of Boston, who had moved to America to get away from the state religion of England and established one of their own instead, steadfastly refused to give him any land. He retaliated by appropriating a corner of Isaac Johnson's old garden and building his chapel next to the graveyard. It was rebuilt in 1749 of hand-cut, local, granite boulders. In the years before the Revolution, because it was the first Episcopal church in New England and named King's Chapel, it became a place singled out for special Royal favor. Queen Anne donated vestments for the clergy, James II financed its pulpit, George III donated its silver communion service and William and Mary presented it with a new communion table and chancel tablets. Accordingly, during the Revolution, it became a place best avoided and its name was even changed to Stone Chapel. Fortunately, the patriots did not bother to cleanse the interior of the Royal gifts, which are still there. But they did drive the Episcopalians out and the chapel, known as King's Chapel once more, became America's first Unitarian/Universalist church after the War of Independence was over.

The Freedom Trail's next landmark is the Old Granary Burying Ground, named for a huge barn that once overlooked the site. It was a storehouse for wheat and corn held there to be sold to the poor in time of famine. Unfortunately, most of its contents went to feed mice and weevils and the building was removed in 1809. The burying ground was there first and, over time, it became the last resting place for three signatories of the Declaration of Independence, eight governors and the immortal Elizabeth Vergoose.

Elizabeth was the second wife of Isaac Vergoose, whose first wife, Mary went to her reward when he was fifty-five, leaving him with ten children to raise. He solved the problem by marrying Elizabeth Foster, a strong young woman of twenty-seven who seemed to have a way with children. Before Isaac died, fifteen years later, she had presented him with ten more, which inspired her to write a little jingle about an old woman who lived in a shoe and "had so many children she didn't know what to do." One of those children, her daughter Elizabeth, married a printer, Thomas Fleet, and had no less than fourteen children of her own. Grandma, who had considerable experience with youngsters, moved in to help take care of them. She amused them, and herself, by reciting little rhymes which her son-in-law eventually published in a little book that is still in print after all these years. By the time the old woman died at the age of ninety-two, her name had been shortened to Goose and, well, you know the rest.

It is believed she was buried in the Old Granary, but the headstone that people claim is hers carries the name "Mary Goose," old Isaac's first wife who, with ten children to her credit surely deserves to be called "Mother." The headstones, as site indicators, mean little in this graveyard, but they make interesting reading nevertheless. In the early days, people were buried there in a random fashion, usually in tight little family groups. But some years ago, the man with the job of keeping the place neat and orderly took his responsibility a bit too seriously and methodically rearranged the headstones into tidy rows. It made the job of cutting the grass a lot easier, but many purists who wanted literally to believe the words "here lies" were not amused.

On the actual site of the Old Granary itself is Henry Banner's 1809 Park Street Church, which Henry James said was "the most interesting mass of brick and mortar in America." It was where William Lloyd Garrison gave his first anti-slavery speech in 1829 and where the song "America" was first sung in 1832. The intersection of Tremont and Park streets, where the church stands, is still known as "the brimstone corner" because gunpowder was stored there during the War of 1812. In 1884, Mary Baker Eddy gave Sunday afternoon lectures there on the healing powers of Christianity, beginning a movement that became known as Christian Science.

Just up the street is a symbol of a religion of a different sort, almost as important as the Congregational Church in the history of Boston. In 1748, a motion was entertained in the House of Representatives to grace its chamber with a memorial to the codfish, the creature that saved the colony from starvation and provided it with its most important export. John Welsh carved it from a block of pine wood and when the legislature moved to the "new" State House in 1795, the "Sacred Cod" went along. The new building is Charles Bulfinch's masterpiece, especially impressive when compared to the newer wings that were added later. The dome, now covered in gold leaf, was originally copper, provided for the project by Paul Revere.

The State House overlooks Boston Common, which was once the garden of the Reverend William Blaxton, or Blackstone, the original owner of the entire peninsula. When the Puritans arrived he invited them to stay on his land because foul water in Charlestown was killing them off rapidly. They accepted, moved over, renamed Shawmut Boston after the small English town they came from and appropriated the land, but they let Blaxton keep fifty acres of what had all been his. However, he sold it back to them a few months later, for a good price, presumably because he thought the neighborhood was being spoiled. The money to buy Blaxton's fifty acres came from a public subscription and the land became the property of all the people, which it still is. It is known today as Boston Common. Even today, the city is not able to change so much as a blade of grass on it without the approval of the citizens.

The northern section of the Freedom Trail winds under the modern John F. Fitzgerald Expressway – named for one of Boston's more colorful mayors, the grandfather of President John F. Kennedy – and meanders back into the past again in the direction of Paul Revere's House. The house itself was over ninety years old when the silversmith bought it in 1770, and is the oldest still standing in Boston. The house that stood over this site before the fire of 1676 was the home of the great minister Increase Mather and his famous son, Cotton Mather. Their church, the "old" Old North, was just around the corner. But the first house on the Revere plot belonged to Captain Kemble, who was condemned to two hours in the stocks by Puritans for "lewd and viscious behaviour." He had kissed his wife on the front steps of their house on a Sunday, having just returned from a three-year sea voyage. A year later, he was back before the court again; this time his offense was "neglecting his wife and living apart from her." He was whipped again.

The church known as Old North today dates back to 1723 and, except for a few weeks during the Revolution, services have been held there every Sunday since. But it is best known as the place where two lanterns flashed the message to Paul Revere that the British were headed for Concord by sea. It was also where General Gage watched his troops battle the Colonials on nearby Bunker Hill. The 170-foot steeple was blown down in an 1804 hurricane and another storm destroyed the replacement in 1954. But the one that is there today would probably look just right to Paul Revere.

The trail continues on to Copp's Hill Burying Ground, the last resting place of some 10,000 old Bostonians, among them William Copp, a shoemaker who arrived with the first wave of Puritan settlers. Some of the headstones bear scars from the Revolutionary War when British soldiers used them for target practice. The hill was the site of the British batteries that destroyed the little village of Charlestown across the river during the Battle of Bunker Hill. From the top of the hill, it is possible to see the Bunker Hill Monument as well as the masts of the U.S.S *Constitution*, fondly known as "Old Ironsides." This ship met the enemy forty times during the War of 1812 and captured twenty enemy vessels without ever being defeated herself.

The Bunker Hill Monument and "Old Ironsides" are official stops on the Freedom Trail walk, but most visitors opt for driving across the river to see them. It is not a long hike, but it looks as if it might be, and energy must be saved for coming back across the bridge again to the North End, one of the best neighborhoods in Boston for exploring on your own. It is also the best place to get a feel for the history of modern Boston. In the beginning it was the neighborhood of choice for the city's best families who began moving south and west in the 1820s when the Irish put their stamp on the city. By the end of the Civil War, the Irish began moving across the river and into the suburbs and the North End was transformed into an Italian neighborhood. Even after all those years some of the twisty little streets would not appear out of place in Naples. It is an adventure to get lost in any part of the city, but nowhere is getting lost any easier or any more fun than in the North End.

Facing page: the Community Boathouse on the Charles River.

Facing page and below right: the Christian Science Center. Below: Trinity Church reflected in the Hancock Tower (above and overleaf). The Tower itself, a controversial work by Pei and Cobb, suffered various teething troubles, not the least being when 3,500 of its 10,344 windows cracked, scattering shards of glass on the square below and increasing the public's need for the very commodity in which the owners dealt: life insurance. Above right: Custom House Tower from Marine Park. Right: the City Hall, described as "an Aztec temple on a brick desert."

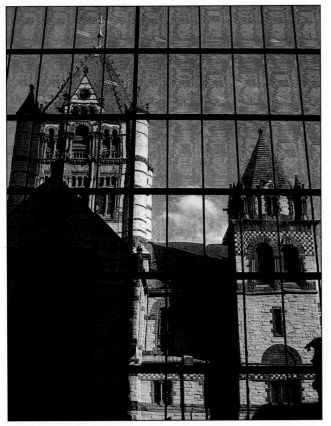

Facing page: (top) the Senate Chamber, and (bottom) Memorial Hall in the Massachusetts State House (these pages). Right: the House of Representatives. The gold-domed building was designed by Charles Bulfinch in 1795 and completed in 1798. Samuel Adams and Paul Revere laid the cornerstone. Paul Revere also provided the copper sheets which originally sheathed the dome until it was recovered with gold leaf in 1861. The portentous "Sacred Cod," a symbol of Boston's early commerce, hangs in the Senate Chamber. Without it being in place the House will not meet. It represents the source of livelihood that sustained and enriched the early Puritan settlers. An abundant source of cod enabled them to forge markets as far afield as the Mediterranean, where the settlers cannily exploited the papal edict that no meat, with the exception of fish, was to be eaten on Fridays.

Below: the Old State House, scene of the Boston Massacre. "Then and there was the first scene of the first act of opposition to the arbitrary claims of Great Britain. Then and there the child Independence was born," according to John Adams. Facing page top: The Globe Corner Bookstore. This store belonged to publishers Ticknor & Fields from 1845 to 1865 and, as the Old Corner Bookstore, was thought of as "the Exchange of Wit, the Rialto of current good things, the hub of the Hub." Facing page bottom: Sweetwater Café and the Zanzibar Club in the Theater District.

These pages and overleaf: Boston Public Garden. This area was wrested from would-be developers in 1837 by Bostonians who wanted the land set aside for horticulture and leisure. It was landscaped in 1860 by George F. Meacham. The Swan Boats are one of the Garden's most famous sights. Strong-legged operators conduct rides in them on the man-made lake constructed out of what was once the swampy marshland of the Charles River. The bronze of George Washington (below) by Thomas Ball has stood in the Public Garden since 1869.

Left: USS Constitution, *moored at the Navy Yard near Bunker Hill. "Nail to the mast her holy flag / Set every threadbare sail / And give her the god of storms / The lightning and the gale!" These impassioned words from Oliver Wendell Holmes' stirring poem* Old Ironsides *saved the ship from being scrapped in 1830. This grand old lady, launched in 1797, ran the gauntlet of many sea battles. On August 19, 1812, she destroyed the British frigate* Guerrière *in thirty minutes. Cannonballs bounced off her hull during the battle, earning her the astonished respect of her British opponents who coined her nickname "Old Ironsides." The sturdy bolts fastening her timbers, and the copper sheathing on her undersides were made by Paul Revere. Below: Long Wharf. Facing page: Rowe's Wharf and the Financial District. Overleaf:* Beaver II, *moored off Congress Street Bridge. Samuel Adams' cry, "Who knows how tea will mingle with salt water?" inspired a revolutionary brew on the evening of December 16, 1773. From Griffin Wharf, three clippers loaded with chests of English tea were relieved of their cargo, which was tipped into Boston Harbor.* Beaver II, *a Danish brig, was launched in 1908 and has been fitted out as one of the original three tea clippers of the Tea Party incident.*

JAMES HOOK + CO. LOBSTERS

Below: the Christian Science Center reflected in its landscaped pool. Right: the Prudential Building at night, and (below right) the Hancock Tower, rising like a huge platinum brick behind Longfellow Bridge, both reflected in the Charles River (overleaf). Bottom right: the man-made lagoon of the Public Garden.

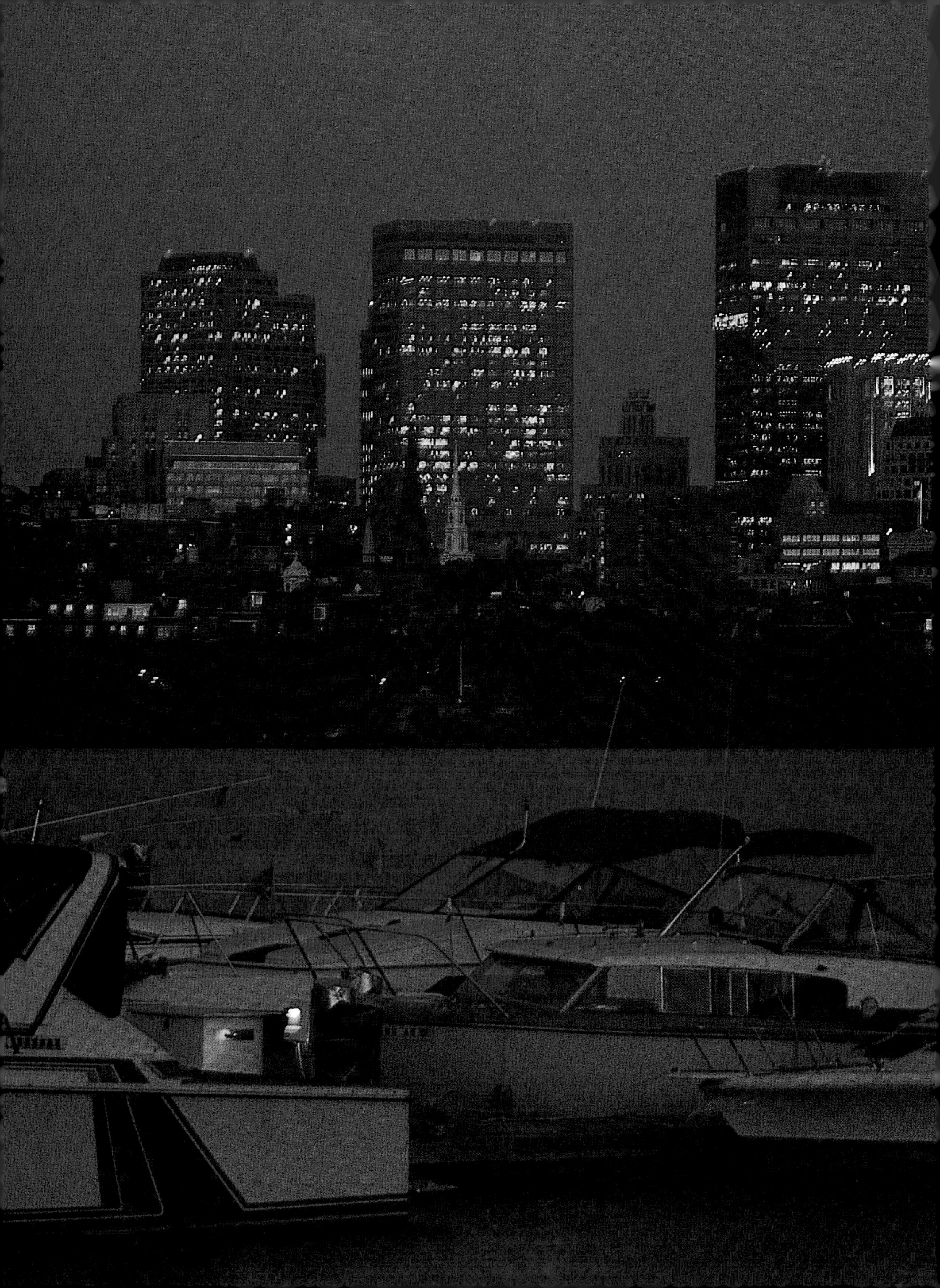

Above and facing page top: the J.F. Kennedy Museum and Library. Kennedy was born in Brookline, a suburb of Boston. Above left: the Christian Science Center. Left: Massachusetts Institute of Technology, Cambridge. Students have likened the MIT academic experience to the shock of trying to take a short drink from a gushing fire hydrant. Below left: the Museum of Fine Arts on Huntington Avenue. Facing page bottom: Harvard's University Hall. Below: the courtyard of the Isabella Stewart Gardner Museum.

Facing page: numbers 11, 13 and 15 Chestnut Street. Numbers 13 to 17 were designed by Charles Bulfinch. From 1863 to 1865, Number 13 was the home of Julia Ward Howe, lyricist of "The Battle Hymn of the Republic." Above right: Louisburg Square. Louisa May Alcott lived at Number 10. Below right: Acorn Street. Oliver Wendell Holmes described Beacon Hill (these pages) as the abode of the "Boston Brahmins." Someone else, less eloquently, remarked that in Boston you could not shoot off a pistol without bringing down the author of a three-volume work.

Below left: the grave of Benjamin Franklin's parents in the Granary Burying Ground (left). Copp's Hill Burying Ground (above left) was founded when the Kings Chapel Ground, once Puritan Isaac Johnson's garden, became full – eventually records noted that "Brother Johnson's garden is getting to be a poor place for vegetables." Above: French's statue of The Minuteman by the North Bridge (overleaf), Concord. Below: Revolutionary Monument and First Parish Church, Lexington Green. Facing page: Bunker Hill Monument, Charlestown.

The original Old West Church (above) was razed by the British in 1775: they suspected the Americans of signaling their troops in Cambridge from its steeple. Below: the interior of Trinity Church (above left). Henry James described Park Street Church (left) as "Perfectly felicitous … the most interesting mass of brick and mortar in America." Facing page top: the interior of the First Church of Christ Scientist in the Christian Science Center (below left). Facing page bottom: inside the new Old South Church. Overleaf: Boston Common.

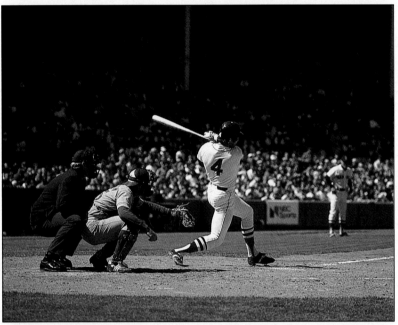

The Boston Red Sox baseball team play as part of the American League at Fenway Stadium (these pages). Paul Fichtenbaum of Sport magazine described Fenway as "a fan's delight, as the players seem a heartbeat away from almost every seat."

Facing page: (top) a yacht skirting Back Bay on the Charles River, and (bottom) Longfellow Bridge. Right: New England Aquarium and Long Wharf. Long Wharf was once so long it began at the Bunch of Grapes Tavern, which John Adams referred to as a "breeding ground for bastards and legislators" and which is now to be found far inland on State Street. Below and above right: the frigate USS Constitution. Above and below right: Beaver II, a replica of one of the "Tea Party" clippers. Overleaf: the Community Boathouse.

Above: Faneuil Hall (below and overleaf) seen across Haymarket (below left). The upper floor of Faneuil Hall, "the Cradle of Liberty," once reverberated to the revolutionary rhetoric of Samuel Adams and James Otis, to name but two. In the impassioned words of Wendell Phillips: "When Liberty is in danger, Faneuil Hall has the right, it is her duty, to strike the key-note for the United States." Left, facing page and overleaf: Quincy Market. Above left: a tiered flower stall outside the Old South Meeting House.

Above: the "Statue of Three Lies" outside University Hall, Harvard (these pages and overleaf), inscribed "John Harvard, Founder, 1638." Harvard was a benefactor, not the founder of the college, which was actually founded in 1636, and nobody knows what he looked like. Left: Dunster House Library. Above left: Harvard Yard. Below left: the Fogg Museum's Naumberg Room. Below: Memorial Hall. Facing page top: Malkin Athletic Center. Facing page bottom: the Faculty Room in University Hall. The faculty list boasts twenty-nine Nobel Laureates.

Above: the J.F. Kennedy birthplace, Brookline. Below: Paul Revere's house, and (left) Longfellow's Wayside Inn, Sudbury, which Longfellow made famous in Tales of a Wayside Inn. *The Wayside (below left), Concord, was home to the Alcotts from 1845 to 1848, and to Hawthorne, who bought the house after publishing* The Blithedale Romance *in 1852. Above left: Buckman Tavern, Lexington, where Minute Men gathered in response to Revere's alarm. Facing page: (top) Longfellow House, Cambridge, and (bottom) Orchard House, Concord.*

These pages: shoppers in Quincy Market on a winter's afternoon. Crickets adorn many restaurant signs, shopping bags and street signs around Quincy Market. This is because when Faneuil gave Boston the Faneuil Hall, he had a large cricket weather vane placed on top of its cupola. During the War of 1812, the word "cricket" became a password and patriot rallying cry in Boston port. Certain strangers who did not recognize this sign or password met untimely ends as spies.

58

These pages: the light-streaked streets of Boston at night. Overleaf: Longfellow Bridge, and (following page) yachts on the gold-woven waves of Boston's Charles River.